Rev Up Your Writing in Fictional Stories

BY YVONNE PEARSON • ILLUSTRATED BY MERNIE GALLAGHER-COLE

The Child's World®

Published by The Child's World®
1980 Lookout Drive • Mankato, MN 56003-1705
800-599-READ • www.childsworld.com

ACKNOWLEDGMENTS
The Child's World®: Mary Berendes, Publishing Director
Red Line Editorial: Editorial direction and production
The Design Lab: Design

PHOTOGRAPHS ©: Shutterstock Images, 6, 18; Tyler Olson/Shutterstock Images, 12

ISBN 9781634070621
LCCN 2014959938

Printed in the United States of America
Mankato, MN
July, 2015
PA02261

ABOUT THE AUTHOR

Yvonne Pearson is a writer and a social worker. She has published books and magazine stories. She writes essays and poems, too. She lives in Minneapolis, Minnesota. She also lives in California near her grandchildren part of each year. Her Web site is www.yvonnepearson.com.

ABOUT THE ILLUSTRATOR

Mernie Gallagher-Cole is a children's book illustrator living in West Chester, Pennsylvania. She loves drawing every day. Her illustrations can also be found on greeting cards, puzzles, e-books, and educational apps.

Table of Contents

CHAPTER ONE

Fiction Is Make-Believe

Do you ever make up stories? Maybe you like to pretend you are an astronaut. Or maybe you are a horseback rider jumping over obstacles. Maybe you like to imagine heroes who save the day.

When made-up stories are written down, they are called fiction. Stories about Spider-Man and Wonder

Woman are fiction. Stories about Amelia Bedelia and Harry Potter are, too.

There are many different kinds of fiction. For example, science fiction imagines what the future will be like. It might have space ships and time travel. Fantasy writing imagines a whole new world. A fantasy world might be a magical place with wizards and dragons. Realistic fiction is a made-up story that seems like it could be true.

Fiction is usually written in **prose**. That means it is written in sentences, not verses. Still, prose often plays with words the way poetry does. For example, prose sometimes uses **rhymes**. That is when two words have the same ending sound. Another example of word play is **onomatopoeia**. That is when a word sounds like the thing it is talking about, such as *buzz* or *tweet*.

There are several forms of fiction. They include short stories, novellas, and novels. A short story is usually about one thing only. So it has a very simple **plot**. You may find short stories in magazines. Some books collect

We read fiction to be entertained. We also read fiction to learn. It can help us understand different experiences.

several stories. "The Tell-Tale Heart" by Edgar Allen Poe is one famous short story.

Novellas are longer than short stories. They have space for more **characters** and more complicated plots. *The Call of the Wild* by Jack London is an example. Novellas may be in a book all by themselves. They may also be in a book with one or two other novellas.

Most people think of novels when they hear the word *fiction*. A novel is long enough to be a whole book by itself. It usually has many characters and complicated plots. The Harry Potter books are examples of novels.

JUSTIN AND GEMMA'S WILD RIDE

Justin and Gemma's mother pointed to the merry-go-round.

"We're kind of old for this, Mom," said Gemma.

"It will be boring," said Justin.

"But this is a very special merry-go-round," said their mother. "Instead of horses, it has dragons."

Justin chose a gray dragon with big wings. Gemma sat next to him on a green dragon with blue wings. The music started, and the dragons moved up and down and around in a circle. Suddenly, the children felt the dragons lift off the ground.

They flew high above the earth, first through a giant cloud and then through a rainbow. The dragons swooped low and rose high. They did flips and twirls. Finally the dragons landed by a river.

Slurp! A sound came from the river. A big, purple fish was drinking from a glass of water.

"What are you looking at?" he asked.

Before the children could answer, a dark cloud came over their heads.

"Buzzzzzz," said the cloud.

"We have to get out of here," yelled Justin.

The dragons quickly lifted back into the air, flying like the wind.

They eased Justin and Gemma back onto the merry-go-round. The music ended, and the children ran back to their mother.

"I hope that wasn't too boring for you," she said.

QUESTIONS
Is this story an example of realistic fiction, science fiction, or fantasy? How do you know? Find two examples of onomatopoeia in this story.

CHAPTER TWO

Elements of Fiction

Fictional stories usually have five elements. Characters are the people the story is about. If you are writing fantasy, characters could also be animals or even plants. **Point of view** is who tells the story. It might be the main character. It might be another character. It might be the author. Plot is what happens in the story.

Setting is where and when the story happens. **Theme** is the meaning or main idea of the story.

Writers have different ways of making characters seem real and interesting. You can try this yourself. Start by dreaming up a character. Decide if it is a girl or a boy. Decide how old your character is. Think about what your character is like. For example, decide if he's serious or funny. Decide if she's strong or weak.

People do not always agree on a book's theme. That is because a book's meaning can be different to each person who reads it.

Then, ask the character questions. For example, you could ask, "What is your favorite food? Do you have a secret? Do you like to play sports?" Imagining the answers can help you understand your character.

Next, you have to help the reader get to know your character. There are three ways you can do this. First, show what the character says, thinks, or does. Second, show what others say about the character. Third, describe what the character looks like.

All of the story's elements add up to the theme. The characters, point of view, plot, and setting create the big idea of the book. A theme might be about courage, friendship, or kindness.

JADE SAVES THE DAY

My name is Jade. Sometimes I get teased because I'm so small. But my best friend, Leah, said I'm great just the way I am. I wasn't so sure about that.

Our class was on a field trip to a climbing wall. I was afraid I would not be able to climb as high as the other kids. What if my arms weren't long enough to reach the handholds? Everybody would laugh at me.

I started to climb the wall, but I couldn't get as high as Jose or Vang. When Jose started to laugh, I scowled hard at him. He pretended to stop, but I could still see him laughing.

Oops! Jose dropped a silver dollar. It flew past my head and rolled into a tiny tunnel by the climbing wall.

When we were done climbing, Jose was sad. He was going to buy his mom a flower with the money he dropped. He tried to crawl into the tunnel, but his body didn't fit. I thought it served him right for laughing. But I knew he was sad, so I crawled into the tunnel and got his money for him.

"Thank you," he said. "I guess it's good to be small sometimes."

QUESTIONS
What is the point of
view in this story?
What things tell us
what Jade is like?
What do you think is the
theme of this story?

CHAPTER THREE

Planning Plot and Setting

Y ou cannot have a story without a plot. Something has to happen.

A plot is like a skeleton. It gives the story its shape. A story's plot must have a beginning, middle, and end. More than one thing usually happens, unless it is a very

short story. There can also be small stories within a bigger story.

A plot should have a **conflict**. That means a character needs to have a problem. By the end of the story, the problem should be resolved.

Every story has to begin in a certain place and at a certain time. A setting might be a farm in summer. Or, it might be on the moon a thousand years from now. It could also be at the bottom of the ocean a thousand years ago.

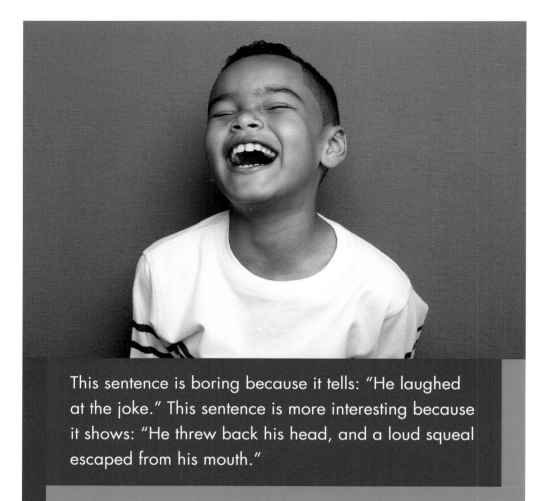

This sentence is boring because it tells: "He laughed at the joke." This sentence is more interesting because it shows: "He threw back his head, and a loud squeal escaped from his mouth."

One important rule of writing fiction is to show, not tell. That means you should not simply tell the reader how your characters feel. Stories are more fun when they explain what is happening with your characters' bodies, the tone of their voices, and the actions they take. That way the reader can feel what is happening in the story.

Here is an example of telling: "James felt sad because his dog was lost." Can you feel James's sadness when you read that sentence? Not really!

Now, turn the page to read an example of showing. Try to notice the difference.

SEARCHING FOR BUTTONS

James shouted his dog's name over and over. "Buttons!" he yelled. "Buttons!"

He looked behind the bushes that grew next to the road. He looked behind the shed in the backyard. He yelled "Buttons!" But his dog did not come. James kicked a stick on the ground. He shoved his hands in his pockets and stomped home.

James spent days searching for Buttons. He asked his father to drive him to the neighbor's house, but Buttons wasn't there. He asked his father to drive him to a park that Buttons loved, but his dog wasn't there. He put up a sign at the grocery store. It said, "Lost Dog. Brown curly hair. Answers to the name of Buttons." But no one called.

James walked into the woods again. He yelled "Buttons" over and over, but there was no Buttons. James sat down in the grass. His stomach hurt. He felt big tears falling down his cheeks.

QUESTIONS
What are the ways that this story shows how James feels? What is the problem or conflict in this story?

TIPS FOR YOUNG WRITERS

1. Read many fictional stories. Make a list of your favorites.

2. Practice writing every day, even if it is just for a few minutes. Keep a special journal for your writing.

3. Make up lots of characters: one who is mean, one who is nice, one who is funny, one who is crazy, and one who is brave.

4. Ask your characters questions. For example, ask what their family is like, or what kind of school they go to, or what they worry about.

5. Make a list of your characters' likes and dislikes.

6. Draw your characters. Maybe your character is tall and skinny, has curly red hair, wears princess costumes, or has a scar on his forehead.

7. Write about things you care about and know.

8. Practice describing settings. Describe the colors, the smells, the sounds, and what things feel like.

9. Think about something fun or exciting that happened in real life. Then, use it as a plot for a story with made-up characters and a made-up setting.

GLOSSARY

characters *(KAR-ik-turz):* Characters are people or animals in a story. Dorothy and Toto are characters in *The Wizard of Oz*.

conflict *(KAHN-flikt):* A conflict is a problem or disagreement. My sister and I had a conflict about who got to wear the astronaut costume.

onomatopoeia *(AH-nuh-MAT-uh-PEE-uh):* Onomatopoeia is when a word sounds like the thing it is talking about. The words *buzz* and *tweet* are examples of onomatopoeia.

plot *(PLOT):* A plot is what happens in a story. The movie had a simple plot: a boy found a map and searched for treasure.

point of view *(POINT of VYOO):* Point of view is who is telling a story. The book was told from the grandpa's point of view, so I knew what it felt like to be an old man.

prose *(PROZE):* Prose is the ordinary language people use to speak or write. Most novels are written in prose, but poetry is not.

resolved *(ri-ZAHLVD):* Resolved means answered or finished. My sister and I resolved our fight by taking turns wearing the astronaut costume.

rhymes *(RIMES):* Rhymes are words that have the same ending sound. *Bat* and *cat* are rhymes.

setting *(SET-ing):* A setting is the place and time where a story happens. The setting for *Goodnight Moon* is a bedroom.

theme *(THEEM):* A theme is the main idea in a story. The theme in many books is the importance of friendship.

TO LEARN MORE

BOOKS

Benke, Karen. *Rip the Page!: Adventures in Creative Writing*. Boston: Roost Books, 2010.

Campbell, Cathy. *The Giggly Guide to Grammar Student Edition*. Shoreham, VT: Discover Writing Press, 2008.

Levine, Gail Carson. *Writing Magic: Creating Stories that Fly*. New York: Collins, 2006.

Traig, Jennifer, ed. *Don't Forget to Write for the Elementary Grades: 50 Enthralling and Effective Writing Lessons*. San Francisco: Jossey-Bass, 2011.

ON THE WEB

Visit our Web site for lots of links about fictional stories:
www.childsworld.com/links

Note to Parents, Teachers, and Librarians: We routinely check our Web links to make sure they're safe, active sites—so encourage your readers to check them out!

INDEX